The Jewish Fake Book

Sima Rabinowitz

Winner
Fourth Annual Elixir Press Poetry Awards

ELIXIR PRESS

The Jewish Fake Book

Grateful acknowledgment is made to the editors and publishers of the following publications in which poems from this manuscript appear:

The Briarcliff Review, "On the Prairie"; *Brooklyn Review*, "The Wrong Law"; *The Cancer Poetry Project*, "Theology"; *Elixir*, "Genealogy"; *Harrington Lesbian Fiction Quarterly*, "If Everything That Burns"; *Minnesota Monthly*, "Biography" (as "Dream Architecture"); *The Neovictorian/Cochlea*, "Yearning for the East"; *New Century Voices 2001*, "French Lesson"; *Poetica*, "My *Yiddishe* Geography"; *The U.S. Latino Review*, "Insomnia."

The Norcroft Writing Residencies, the Minnesota State Arts Board, and SASE: The Write Place and the Jerome Foundation provided generous support for this project.

I am indebted to Sarah Kennedy, judge for the Fourth Annual Elixir Press Poetry Awards.

Many thanks to Carol Evans-Smith for her skill and generosity in producing "On the Second Page." For invaluable help in shaping these pages, figuratively and literally, I am deeply grateful to Ruthann Robson and, always, to Susan Denelsbeck.

ISBN: 1-932418-07-5

Cover Art: Peter Kowler
Cover Concept: Susan Denelsbeck
Cover Layout: Collin Hummel
"On the Second Page" Design: Carol Evans-Smith
Author Photo: Carol Guse

Elixir Press is a non-profit literary organization.

Elixir Press
P. O. Box 18010
Minneapolis, MN 55418
www.elixirpress.com

Table of Contents

III Philosophy

IV The Jewish Fake Book

Foreword

Poetry of reverence may seem an old-fashioned term, but the poems in Sima Rabinowitz's *The Jewish Fake Book* have an abiding concern with the possibilities of divine language as it enters the secular world. From the "exalted syllables" of "Sacrilege" to the "language of luxury" in "French Lesson," this is work that demands attention to all acts of speech and writing. In narrative, lyric, meditation, and prayer, these poems make up a sacred syntax that speaks in startling new ways about the material world.

Rabinowitz's range extends from three-line petition to page-filling prose poem to mini-one-act play, and it may tempt some readers to call her—or dismiss her as—an experimental writer. These poems, however, are explorations, and they reveal again and again that words are (can I say it?) *holy* in whatever form they appear. This is not to suggest that form is arbitrary in this collection; on the contrary, the many types of poem that appear here are testaments to the variety of shapes and modes that the word can make manifest. Rabinowitz is an ambitious poet, willing to risk breaking even the permeable boundaries of contemporary writing by using the traditional strategies of anaphora, embedded metaphor, dialogue, and cataloging to make her poems.

The play between narrative and lyric modes, moreover, lends richness to the collection. She begins in history, both personal and spiritual, and these poems build lives detail by detail. "The Diaspora Cycle" introduces a speaker who constructs herself from the fragments at hand:

> I set out from the wilderness of history
> and camped at the edge of the desert.
> I set out from the edge of the desert
> and stopped by the tablets of stone.
> I set out from the tablets of stone
> and passed by the ten generations.
> I set out from the ten generations
> and entered the city of refuge.
> I set out from the city of refuge
> and unraveled the scroll of myself.

This speaker, however, is not a faceless "universal I"; she is a character revealed through the book's concern with gender identity and family tradition. "Genealogy," the title poem of Part I, asks the book's central question(s):

> What does it mean:
> to be the daughter of women exiled by custom
> from tenderness
> to be the daughter of men banished by circumstance
> from second chances
> to be the grandchild of duty, the offspring
> of obligation
> to be the sister of daughters who mothered themselves
> to be mother to none?

The speaker claims that a "holy war between the literal … and the … allegorical" is "in [her] blood" and so when she imagines "Biography" as "psalm, as story," it should come as no surprise. Song and chronicle are not mutually exclusive; they are, in fact, mutually illuminating.

That illumination, that resonance, often happens through incrementally morphing repetition, an accrual of meaning that becomes incantatory. The book opens with "Sacrilege," a list poem that echoes through the poems that follow it. It asks for "One book" again and again, from "One book — receptacle, holograph" to "One book — eternal life." Is it too much to ask? The "One Hundred and Forty-Seven Negative Confessions" seem to answer no(yes); "the alphabet," it asserts, "is a silent continent," but the speaker is "a country of small confessions." These confessions unsay themselves and each other, reaching for a truth that only paradox can encompass: "I do not covet ancient metaphors (*I am utterly vanquished before a star*)." Housed in the mortal body, speech is always in danger of unsaying itself; though the body itself is "light," the speaker's skin is the "Boundary that separates/ The world above from the world below."

Despite the recognition of such self-contradiction, however, speech still strives toward truth. Sima Rabinowitz's abiding awareness that language and the created world—what we recognize as *real*— rests in *The Jewish Fake Book*'s revelation of tropes, without which we cannot think and therefore cannot exist. Tenor and vehicle, in this "palace of metaphor," intersect, interpenetrate until even grammar cannot contain it. "Infinitives split into fragrant worlds" in these complex poems and every word multiplies as it turns on itself:

> In a Universe where every word
> is an act and every act
> affects the whole of Creation,
> a single utterance shifts the axis
>
> sane   obsessed
> profane   blessed

Sarah Kennedy

Sacrilege

One book — that's all I ask.
One book — receptacle, holograph.
One book — not an invocation, evocation, emendation.
One book — slender as the desert.
One book — the same language and the same words.
One book — not a decree.
One book — in which I am blameless.
One book — revealed in a city of fire, no thicket of reeds.
One book — not a homily.
One book — of water, wine, and milk.
One book — transcribed in a fever of salt, of rhyme.
One book — not a prophecy.
One book — graven, graven, graven.
One book — the color of beets in the ground.
One book — not a proverb.
One book — where only rhythm is sacred.
One book — the fruit of the fig tree, precise and unalterable.
One book — the story of a body in motion.
One book — exalted syllables.
One book — not a slate of miracles.
One book — torn from trembling fingertips.
One book — irreverent.
One book — not vanity, but providence.
One book — abstract of an abstract.
One book — eternal life.

I

Genealogy

The Diaspora Cycle

One

It was a long time in the wilderness. Perhaps not forty years.
Perhaps not the wilderness of wild beasts,
a hand-sewn tent barely cover from the winds.
More like the drawn, empty face of strangers,
or curiosity's well-intentioned mispronunciations.
More like the unsolicited, almost secular greeting
for a feast at someone else's table.
More like misshapen stars, a wrinkled scroll,
odd-numbered candles. Artifacts of hasty judgment.
More like contraband prayers and proverbs,
jewels once pressed to the roofs of our mouths with cautious tongues,
now wholesale slogans or the sloppy refrain of a popular song.
More like the incidental fasts that lasted weeks and weeks.
We did not plan to be repentant:
but there was nothing on the platter we could eat.

Two

My past has no vowels.
Only memory.
Only absence of memories.

Three

Where there was no story
or where the story was
that there was no story
there were rules:
the blood, the oil, the smoke on the altar,
the hawk, the kite, the heron, the owl,
the sash and tunic,
the grapes that have fallen to the ground.
The clay pot, the bronze bowl
do not remind me of mirrors.
I do not know how to read the numerals
in the covenant of weights and measures.

Four

I set out from the wilderness of history
and camped at the edge of the desert.
I set out from the edge of the desert
and stopped by the tablets of stone.
I set out from the tablets of stone
and passed by the ten generations.
I set out from the ten generations
and entered the city of refuge.
I set out from the city of refuge
and unraveled the scroll of myself.

Five

There was, finally, the exodus,
flight from diminished expectation,
from the grammar of silence,
untangling the root letters,
unlearning, renaming,
figuring out how not to be chosen — but to choose.

Genealogy

(1)
What does it mean:
to be the daughter of women exiled by custom
                                    from tenderness
to be the daughter of men banished by circumstance
                                    from second chances
to be the grandchild of duty, the offspring
                                    of obligation
to be the sister of daughters who mothered themselves
to be mother to none?

(2)
A generation of hand-me-downs had finally worn thin
                                    worn out
and still we walked around as if we had our blouses
                                    on backwards
collars upside down.
It wasn't that we didn't own anything,
only that nothing belonged to us.
Maybe nobody noticed our lunch bags
                                    smelled of garlic.
Maybe they did.

(3)
Later we were mistaken for other lost tribes
or the enemy-of-the-week from the evening news.
And there were days I forgot which sea
                                    I'd crossed
to be free of the burden of mistaken identity.
From my father I inherited a fear
                                    of the known.
From my mother a fear
                                    of the unknown.
There is only who we have not become
to tell us who we were.

Wild Relatives

[The undomesticated varieties, found in nature,
of genetically modified seeds.]

Mine include a sister who slapped my cheek
until a streak, hot pink resolution,
bloomed and blistered, once and finally, between us.
We were arguing about dirt.
How much it costs to get rid of it.

So I deducted the price of the cookies, she explains
after I complained, naturally, *to the management.*

How many cookies did they take? (I try to ascertain
the housecleaners' motives.)

I'm not sure, three or four, a half dozen. It's the principle.

Which might be hunger, I conclude.

That's when our conflict blossoms into a feud.
You're so judgmental it makes me sick, she spits from the door
where she clutches cab fare in one guilty palm
and the daughter she's brought halfway across the country
for show (and tell) in the other.
It's the middle of the night
and the baby is too stunned or too sleepy to cry out.

There's also a second cousin, once removed,
who hurled himself, during rush hour,
under the métro at the Sherbrooke station.
(Or was it Place-des-Arts?)
February 14, 1967, after phoning his sister
to wish her, a few days early, a *happy, happy birthday.*

Years later I spent ten months in Montréal
where I visited his parents every weekend,
rode the train from Bonaventure to Jarry.
(Or was it Frontenac?)
Lunch was always cold borsht and cold fish,
gelled and shimmering like their memory of Norman
poised above the innocent tracks on Valentine's Day.

Just those two, really. O.K., perhaps a third,
my brother's wife who corrects us
friend, as if it were two syllables,
fer-end, she says of the woman
with whom her mother shared
forty years and four houses in four states,
the aftermath of too many rounds of chemo
to count and a Pekinese named Gertrude.

There — only three. Not counting
my mother's uncle George
who could hardly be considered wild
since for five decades he refused to leave
the confines of his one-room walk-up
on the Lower East Side. She visited him
the summer after his sister (my grandmother) died.

Did you bring the secret formula? he asked her.
Of course, she said.
She put the coffeecake she baked
by the hot plate in the corner.

French Lesson

It was the language of luxury (*carte
Blanche*) and of indifference (*comme çi, comme ça*).
Not the vulgar, guttural, crude patois
Of the severed tongues of which we were part.
Our romance with the foreign meant obeying
The sounds of understatement, not excess,
Seductive, though subdued — that silent s.
Not like the *sturm und drang* of speech decaying.

Sometimes we practiced turning a deaf ear
To *tsouris, meshuginah*, and *schmata*,
To rhymed advice so coarse
We'd cringe to think that anyone would hear,
"Everything's *farblunjet*"— (what a *faux pas*).
We said *adieu* to that and no remorse.

On the Prairie

All the formulas desert me here:

     arid instructions
     vast sea of rejoinders
     dense acrostics waiting for a scythe
          to slice and shuffle their patterns
     parcels of syllogisms, corners bound and tied
     territory that is allegory
     landscape of commentary, all context
          and ragged margins
     shoreline, sand and silt, rescued waters,
          ark of fables.

Here is only the broad sky:

     where letters fly forward, wings clipped, holding their breath,
     where pronouns bend sideways in the wind
     and even the spine of the *I* curves
     to meet the unearthly green ground.

If this is not exile, what is?
Where is my wilderness — that great and terrible house?

Guide of the Perplexed

"His masters claimed to be able to give one hundred and twenty interpretations of this phrase, whose literal meaning is, however, totally clear."
Marc-Alain Ouaknin, *The Burnt Book*

It's in my blood. Argument, debate —
— that holy war between the literal,
trash heap of supplies and utensils, our common bread,
and the shining armor of the allegorical.

But what, I want to know, could be more complex,
than a thorn and thistle,
or the seamless shell of the coriander seed?

And what could be more singular, more straightforward,
than a name or numeral turned inside out
to reveal itself in the light between layers?

Biography

for Sari Kraus (1901-1993)

Many nights I sleep the organized
predictable sleep of the middle-aged,
dream the bureaucrat's measured dream of
habit and management. The week's
responsibilities spine to spine, horizontal harmony,
labeled, ordered, transparent.
The sleep of someone too inflexible to sleep afraid,
to conjure animal shapes in seamless rooms,
shapeless sound, disembodied shrieks and chanting.
But tonight I know she is dying — and as I sleep
a great library burns:
wrists, hands, fingers, distended grip
shelves and pillars until they collapse,
everywhere the hiss of paper tearing,
fragile as flesh,
and all the pieces falling, falling,
words and stone.
Towers and tables, sonnets and indices,
fiery collage of maps and catalogues and moaning
in the wild night air.
Dictionaries and history books, that relentless fiction,
covers scarred, ink drips scalded from flame
to frozen earth.
Someone recites the alphabet,
the sound of forgetting.
When I wake, with her name in my clenched fist,
I imagine her as psalm, as story.

Permutations — The Science of Mysticism

1 Chemistry

Looking down through the mire
it is as if my feet have dissolved
                    into the soil
aluminum, calcium, potassium,
the patterns replacing themselves
(with less of themselves)
liquid rising to bathe
ankles, shins, thighs, hips,
waist, wrists, chest, chin
                    water, water
the wet sounds drown
gums, teeth, lips…feet.
Feet — I can see my feet —
the trance undone, eroded
by naming or by the impulse,
reckless and inevitable,
                    to swallow.

2 Heredity

As far as I know
there have been no
mystics in our family
(on either side) —
a vintner, a kosher butcher,
an unemployed janitor in Schenectady —
no mystics.

This (*this* alone) doesn't worry me.
What, belief notwithstanding,
is there to stop me
from trying?

The rituals — innate, secret — come naturally
counting
counting counting
counting counting counting
counting counting counting counting
counting counting counting counting counting
counting counting counting counting counting counting counting

a single figure swells to fill
my field of vision

street lights between this corner and the next, beige squares
in the linoleum, teal squares in the linoleum, beats between
the crow's mean A flat, slats in the broad wood blinds, miles
from here to here (or is it there?) and back, concrete steps (up
and down), limp shadows in a bowl of soup, white squares in
the linoleum, petals on a pale yellow moss rose, slivers of carrot,
minutes, days, hours, weeks typing (retyping) this list, half-moons
of onion, (down and up), clouds of potato, days since the last rain,
and the rain before that, jars facing left on the shelf, jars facing
right, street lights between this corner and the next, beige squares

The north wind of obsession
— water from breath —
dutifully (joyfully) douses the sums
and I begin
again.

And that rabbi who lost his mind
gazing at the Source of perfection?
Listen, only a crazy person craves Paradise
stray purposes accounted for,
numbers banished,
the nightmare absence
of compulsion.

3   Anatomy

From under the Arms of the Universe
bound on four sides and so also unrestrained,
the numbers (as letters) and letters (as numbers)
grope with all ten fingers
deciding between Heights and Depths.
I am not what I am not I but
limb by limb
vowel by vowel
                    Nothing
transparent as breath.
        chant-breathe; chant-breathe; chant-breathe; chant-breathe;
        breathe, breathe, breathe, breath...

...I have paid too much attention
and not enough...
the image of my-self as no-self
becoming, by definition in (some) sense
                    a body of ideas.
I gain what I gave up
and must begin again.

4   Pathology

You can't tell anyone, of course.
But even if a modest revelation
were permitted what would you say?
Hey, great news:

        I lost my feet halfway through the alphabet?
        I misplaced my left hand. Or was it my right?
        I forgot my jaw, the roof of my mouth, the length of my tongue.

It's the length of my (pre) occupation
that is unknowable
which is the point and also not the point
because I have to live (to write)

deciding between Heights and Depths
as if I don't know they (don't) exist.

As if I don't have ceilings, walls, gardens
                    to enumerate.
As if I don't have numberless Worlds
                    to populate
with endless pairs of phonemes
and the dust of seven earths.

In a Universe where every word
is an act and every act
affects the whole of Creation,
a single utterance shifts the axis
                    sane   obsessed
                    profane   blessed.

I Heard a Language That I Knew Not

Sing joyously — Psalms (81)

Where there are numbers
but no counting
where there are letters
but no words
where there is light
but no moon
night, but no river

where there is sand
but no earth
earth, but no rock

where there is breath
but no air
air, but no shadow

where there are numbers
no words
where there are letters
no counting
where there is sand
but no air
where there is rock
but no shadow

river, but no moon

where there is sky
but no breath
shadow, but no light

sing   for   there   is   music.

Yearning for the East

It's not as if I haven't tried
to recover that golden territory
                   of heroes and heretics.
The land of first sun, first moon, first sea,
the kingdom of yearning.
And let's face it — every place is west of somewhere
                   even here.
It would be, dare I say it, a blessing
to desire a past as specific
as a bracelet of coarse salt encircling
                   a startled wrist,
the reflection of hot, pink stone, smooth as the cornea,
                   lighting the hills and ladders,
the scent of aloes, myrrh, and cinnamon rising from
                   caves and tunnels at dusk.

I'd sacrifice this warm skin, this animal heart,
for one night of dreaming backwards,
the letters of the secret books
unraveling — one long, shimmering strand
— reforming right to left and right again.
To wake, then, with the words etched in flame
                   on my pillow.
To move like a star in the river.
To follow the pillars of cloud, pillars of fire —
                   — toward sacred ground.

Other Egypts

The far-flung sparks of the broken vessel
the misplaced light of interpretation —
I was, I'll admit it, greedy for the facts.
At first, anyway.
Names and dates, numbers and letters
stacked on top of each other,
a genetics of abundance,
small chemical epiphanies.
The volume of data delighted me.

Later I was compelled by analogies,
cross references, allegory,
the dense translation
from earth to heaven and back,
sacred garden of suggestions.
And later still by the way the words meant
everything or nothing,
how I could make them mean anything I wanted
simply by inverting the symbols,
how they added up to more or less
of what I already knew.

And I broke the rules, coveted
what already belonged to me.
I hoarded the little fragments,
the names of people, places, things,
and best of all, the ecstatic titles of ancient books:
The Bed of Spices, The Gate of Wisdom, The Book of Destiny.
I gathered the exotic syllables in cupped palms
and between the covers of my notebooks,
color-coded, spiral-bound,
tangible evidence of the past,
the quest for a subject to manipulate.

It was not selfish so much as dishonest
this lust for synonyms.
But I had convinced myself
the work was deciphering antiquity.
The riddle of myself left undiscovered:
I was not the text in question.

It was the most exquisite exile.
And wasn't I, after all, the offspring
of silence, of absence, the unrevealed?
I was meant to miss my own story:
Sarah's years unnumbered,
Dina's unblessed daughters,
Esther's veiled face.
My endless notebooks, another pillar of salt.

But when, after a time unmeasured,
I assembled the shards of history,
I saw how I had concealed the shape of my longing.
And the lost sparks were scattered still
uncounted, homeless.

My *Yiddishe* Geography

1. *Treyf* — A Pennsylvania Story

She had to climb not once, but twice, nervous and naked, into the tepid pool with three somber, bearded, fully clothed men looking on, heads covered, eyes alight on the water's surface. Twice, not for reasons of ritual, but to rectify an error — one of the rabbis said he wasn't sure her fingertips had been completely immersed, he thought he'd seen a thin crescent of pink floating above the water. I was surprised she didn't give up the project altogether at that point. Just trying to keep a kosher kitchen in our rural Pennsylvania town where the only grocery store was brimming with sausage, bratwurst, bacon, canned pork and beans, and freezers full of round, pink hams for Sunday dinner, was hard enough. True, she'd already given up meat, had been a vegetarian for years, but I knew it wasn't what she was giving up, but what she was getting that mattered for her conversion. And that was Noam's baby, something the rabbis, standing like lecherous statues at the edge of the *mikveh*, did not know.

How she and Noam managed to make that baby is something of a miracle. The *frum* family with whom she stayed in Baltimore every weekend for worship, study, and lessons in Orthodox family life certainly never left her alone with a man, let alone her future husband. Noam never came to Pennsylvania to visit during the week: he was much too busy at the *yeshiva*. And it was truly, as far as I could tell, his commitment, his dedication, his passion for tradition and rigorous religious practice that attracted her to him. I asked her what it meant, in terms of this tradition, his having a baby with a Christian woman he wasn't married to. She told me Noam said nothing in the law prohibited a Jewish man from having relations with a non-Jewish woman, as long as she wasn't married. If she were Jewish or married that would be forbidden, of course. She didn't know herself if what he was telling her was really quite right, but after all, that's why she was studying now, wasn't it, to marry, have his baby, and become a good Jew, a religious Jew. *You should follow our example*, she told me. *The Torah is a beautiful book. Come with me to Baltimore, join our congregation, study... This is your tradition*, she admonished, *you should honor it. It belongs to you and soon it will belong to me, too.* I certainly didn't know if what Noam had told her was true or not, but either way it was as distasteful to me as the pickled pig's feet on the shelf at GIANT FOODS down the street.

After she lost the baby, Noam moved to Tel Aviv with an Orthodox woman he met through a colleague at the *yeshiva*. It was six weeks before the wedding and since they weren't married yet there was no need for a *get*.

2. *Narishkeit* — A Minnesota Play

The time is the present. The place is the equipment and supply room of a corporate office in St. Paul, Minnesota.

Me: Hi, how are you?
Him: Good. How are you?
Me: Fine.

(Silence — the only sound is the drone of the copy machine.)

Him: What are you again?
Me: What?
Him: What are you?
Me: What am I?
Him: You know, what nationality?
Me: You mean where did my grandparents come from?
Him: Yeah, I guess.
Me: Hungary and Russia. But, that was a long time ago.
Him: That's not what I meant.
Me: I'm not sure what you're asking me.
Him: Well, I mean you're Jewish, right?
Me: That's not a nationality.
Him: *(In a breezy fashion)* Sure it is.
Me: *(Firmly)* No, it isn't.
Him: Yes, it is. What about Israel?
Me: People from Israel are Israelis, that's their nationality. My family's not from Israel.

Him: But you're Hebrew.

Me: There is no Hebrew nationality. Hebrew is a language. Israeli is a nationality. Jewish is someone who practices Judaism. That's a religion.

(Silence — the only sound is the drone of the copy machine.)

Him: Yeah, but not really. I mean what about the food and everything.

Me: *(Slowly)* What food?

Him: You know, bagels and all that other stuff, that fish.

Me: *Gefillte* fish?

Him: Yeah, that's what I mean, and that language.

Me: You mean Yiddish.

Him: Yeah, I guess. Yeah, that's what I mean. *(Beat)* So do you speak Yiddish or Hebrew at home?

Me: *(Under her breath)* Oif a nar iz kain kasheh nit tsu fregen un kain pshat nit tsu zogen. *(You should not ask a fool a question nor give him an explanation.)*

3. *Gonif* — An Ohio Poem

Ohio poet, you stole the jokes.
You stole the puns.
You stole the metaphors.

Stole a river of myths.
Sea of stories.
History.

There's a word in Yiddish for who you are,
     for what you've done —
     — more than one.

II

Theology

In the *Tzitzit* Laboratory

For centuries they have divined
the origins of the bluest blue:
the snail's blue, *tekhelet*, the holy blue.
Blue of first light.
Blue of a desert sun.
Sovereign blue of ancient cords and molecules.
Blue that swallows up our enemies
and leaves the ground gaping, purple.

Blue as the improbable vowel
bobbing beneath the blue-black sea
that swells, square by square,
towards a parchment shore,
as it spells out the laws and formulas
for everything (including blue).
Blue as the ink of nine thousand mollusks,
every seventy years,
curled, dextral, in the sand,
innocent of meaning.

No ordinary blue —
our earthly portion.
Blue as the source of sacred chemistry.
Blue as the tyranny of exactitude,
as the science of the righteous.

What We Prayed For - 1

The lost seasons
believing, not

believing.

What We Prayed For - 2

Believe me — I knew it wouldn't work.
I knew what I was up against.
All those unsung praises,
infinitives split into fragrant worlds.

What can I say? I was desperate,
shameless, bended knee, the whole stooped effort.

You don't need to know what I asked for,
only that I asked.

What We Prayed For - 3

The shelves buckled under
the weight of books we read

to refute: *my people gone
into exile for want of knowledge.*

We saw what they did
not say, these books. Still, harvest

to harvest we gathered their
rotting between cupped palms.

What We Prayed For - 4

Know this:
I thought of everything
as not-a-prayer.

Beyond Uranium

Lise Meitner (1878–1968) of Vienna was an experimental physicist.
In 1938, she fled the Berlin laboratory where she had been employed.
Despite her fundamental contributions to the field of nuclear physics,
her biography remains little known.

I had made the particular heat
that's derived of division my life's work,
the fission of the cell from (it) self
the burn and thunder at the core,
that something from nothing, nothing we could see,
the hot, white light of dispersion,
the spark and recombination.
Does it matter that I thought it was one thing,
and it turned out to be another?
Has any element ended up to be what it was
when we started?

Thirty fiery years in the lab, living from
notebook to notebook, theorem to theorem
ripe decades of experiment, intimate investigation,
hand to the heart (of the problem),
heart on fire (with the solution).
And still I never once suspected the conclusion:
that eventually I, too, could be severed
from the center of (my) self, split from the body
of the work, from the doing, the discovery,
from all our beautiful results,
cast off not only from urgent purpose,
from usefulness, but also from my family,
the one that I was given and the one I had created,
peers and colleagues, their wives and children.

Reduced and fragmented,
not to be remade as multiple or more,
like the atoms in their naïve exuberance,
but instead merely diminished,
stripped of everything,
no longer a person, not even an Austrian,
simply a forbidden name, suppressed past,
isolated and homeless,
without my catalogues and apparatus,
without relations, without relationships,
without science.

In Stockholm, at fifty-nine, I survived
on a student's stipend, lean as the nucleus of absent friends.
I learned a meaner discipline, loneliness, desertion,
so distraught by this unthinkable betrayal
I could not think, sometimes, to be glad for
my survivor's fate, and this was hardly living,
these blank days, my confidence confiscated
with the books and laboratory notes,
the feather bed, my mother's silver.
I stood alone with empty hands,
far from my scientific things,
instruments of invention and identity.

Just being a woman was half-a-crime
at the Nobel Institute. And the news
from abroad was evidence that some rank
and sinister mechanism expected
to govern the universe. Still, I kept my faith
in the natural order of things, the correspondence
between laws and substances, precepts and reactions,
what we can observe and what is meant to happen.

In the end, I was invited to return to Berlin,
but I chose, instead, my immigrant status.
By then I understood, despite the elemental truths
we had spent a lifetime demonstrating —

— what has been ruptured at its source
can never be made whole again.

Theology

The language for speaking to and about God is metaphoric,
says the feminist Talmudic scholar.
I'd be interested in a more direct approach myself,
though I have to say I can understand
the appeal of speaking in tongues,
consonants glued together like oatmeal or aspic,
sticky and thick with confidence,
no place for puns, or analogies, or parody,
so utterly illogical, they're believable —
                                    — or, at least, indisputable.

God's name is God,
says a little girl to her mother in the coffee shop on 54th and
Lyndale.
It's directness I crave, yes, specificity, some granite evidence
when you tell me, dead metaphor:
                    It's the size of a grapefruit.
                    I'll have to do another round of chemo.
Not something or someone to accuse necessarily,
but a name less precise and more accurate,
a way to call attention to the rock solid face of grief.

Hapaxlegomena

one
once
only

as in revelation

Golan Heights Judea Bassa Samaria Jezreel
Khisas Ghabisiyya Birwa Gaza Metulla Jordan
Abu Zureik Eilat Rosh Hanikra Sasa Sharon
Haifa Tel Aviv Abuna Shefela Mt. Meron Wadi
Difla Galilee Ajjur Akbara Acre Sodom Ein
al-Tine Negev Jaffa Haifa Shefar-Am Jerusalem
Gamla Mishmar Haemeq Petakh
Tikvah Zir'in Mount Gerizim
Nazareth Qastal Wadi 'Ara
Bethlehem Dawaima Sinai

Hebron Rana Deir Yasin Safed Tiberias
Sataf Nahal Arbel West Bank Iqrit Nablus
Qalquilya al-Faluja Latroun Beisan Kafr
Birim Ramla Ofra Beersheba Ramallah
Netanya Tulkarm Caesarea Zikhron Yaakov
Hadera Yazur Afula Nahariya Kiriyat
Shemona Katzrin Ein Hawd
Rehovot Kfar Sava Yanua
Lydda Mt. Carmel Saffuriyya
Mount Hermon Ashkelon

occupation
profession
profess
occupy
pre-occupied

In the settlement of Natzarim, Gaza Strip, a father releases the empty vessel of his son from his arms. As the breath leaves the small boy's body, the stones slip from his fist. His mother wails, to those who did this, I say may you burn.

On the second page you will learn what you need to know for the sake of peace.

The Holy One found no vessel that could contain Israel's blessing except peace.

settle-ment
to settle
an argument
to settle
for less
to settle
to agree
to settle
to decide

Our masters taught to prevent enmity one may change something that has been said.

We are obliged to remove the Arabic names for reasons of state. Just as we do not recognize the Arab's political ownership of the land, so we also do not recognize his (her?) ownership of the names.

state
state of being
state a fact
state-ment
to make
a statement

He (She?) who causes the giving of charity, confers peace.

designate
to name
to assign duties
duty
responsibility

A House in which there is dissension will be destroyed in the end.

The first house (in Abu Kabir) is every house. The first village (in al-Khisas) is every village.

refuge
refu(s)e
refugee

Our masters taught some forbidden acts may be permitted to prevent enmity.

Aliyah
(to immigrate)
to ascend
to rise above

The mountains and valleys, villages and roads, olive trees and citrus groves. The land remembers our undoing, undoing. Millions of grieving acres, unblossoming.

endure
to suffer
to survive

Reproof leads to peace and peace that has no reproof with it, is not peace.

re-proof
to prove
again
and
again

The world endures because of three things, justice, truth, and peace.

Any controversy that is carried on for Heaven's sake will, in the end, be of lasting worth, but only that which is carried on for Heaven's sake will, in the end, be of lasting worth. What controversy was for Heaven's sake? In the end? To what end? To end what? When He (She?) made peace, He (She?) created everything. Every. Thing. Abundant peace. Abundant. Abound. Bound. Bind. Oblige. Obligation. Boundary. Bound-less. Bound to the second page.

The Wrong Law

*"If it were true, and it is not, my wife is awaiting a horrible end
for having typed a few notes!"*

**Ethel Rosenberg quoting Julius Rosenberg
in a letter to her sons' guardians
June 8-9, 1953, Sing Sing Prison**

I'm not going to tell you
what you want to know.
Not on either count.
As for the first thing — there's my promise to Julie
(*courage, confidence, perspective*).
And as for the other, well — it goes against the laws of nature.

It shouldn't surprise me, I suppose,
that even after all these years
you're still asking the wrong questions,
mistaking attitude for evidence.

What I will you tell is this:
I did not choose silence to protect a secret.
I did not speak because no one
could understand what I had to say:

      Not about the chain reaction
      my brother's treason set in motion.

      Not about the way my mother's betrayal
      imploded every notion of love in our small (unoffending) Jewish family.

      Not about that coldwater prison on Sheriff Street
      where, as a girl, I was captive to a tradition I never lost faith in.

      Not about my own explosive baby boy
      whose tantrums still light up the night sky over Ossining.

Not about the appeals, pleas really, we made
our whole (short) long lives.
Me to artistry, ideology, and finally psychotherapy.
Julius first to one Jewish bible and then to the other.
Not about the music that erupted from my swollen throat,
that hot, frothy song leaking over and under the mesh and steel.

Not about the numbers (110-510) that branded my letters
(to Julie, to the boys)
and burned in my breast and brain, if not on my wrist.

Not about the Sabbath-at-sunset debate, execution of the wrong law,
conspiracy of ancient rules and modern rites.

Not about my unstoppable heart (*this woman is still alive*)
its implausible contents throbbing,
throbbing inside that imperfect holding cell, my body.

One Hundred and Forty-Seven Negative Confessions

After reading José V. Malcioln, on
The African Origins of Modern Judaism

Hear (oh, Israel) — the alphabet is a silent continent.
And I, I am a country of small confessions:

I did not steal the title of this book. Or the book inside this book.

Before I wrote her name, I did not consider (darkest) Eve my sister.

I crossed a sea to reach this list.

I have never loved the idea of God. god. A God. gods. A God. G-d. G(o)od.

I will not make a false confession.

I do not covet ancient metaphors (*I am utterly vanquished before a star*)

I do (not) transgress in order to confess.

When a Jew professes (she confesses).

This is the only confession I will devote to transgression.

I was (not) surprised to learn the commandments
had betrayed themselves in their conception.
What father does not imagine other progeny?

I do not covet the word Africa.

This is not a poem about Africa.

I decided not to confess (about Africa).

I do (not) understand what Africa has to do with these confessions.

I am not ashamed to say I am afraid of Africa.

I did not steal the phrase *like the depths of my Africa.*

These confessions are (not) negative.

I am (not) privileged to make this confession.

Be humble before all persons.

I am not indebted to my own confusion (for this poem).

I would not say that Africa is a metaphor.

I did not abandon these confessions for days at a time hoping (praying)
the word Africa would disappear.

These confessions are not dangerous.

This is the only confession I will devote to hate.

Hatred of one's fellow human beings will ruin a person's life.

I am not tired of confessing. Yet. Already.

I have (already) atoned for every transgression.
                                        (One day each year).

I have (never) claimed a whole nation's transgressions as my own.
                                        (Each day, every year).

I do not covet the one who has already completed her confession.

I have never been in love with my own white(ness).

I do (not), of course, know the Yiddish (word) for black (people)
or the Hebrew (word) for blackest Egypt.

I did not steal the words *what would I do white?*

I have never imagined myself as Africa.

I am not afraid of (my) imagination.

I am not afraid of Africa.

I am not indebted to my own fear (for this poem).

This is the last confession I will devote to fear.

It did not take ten commandments to reach Africa.

The world was created by ten utterances.

I did not learn by heart (only) nine.

These confessions are not sacrilegious.

I am (not) ashamed of these confessions.

I will not justify my confusion. I mean confession.

I do (not) know who she is, sister Africa.

I have never pretended to be Africa.

This is the last confession I will devote to pretense.

These confessions are (not) irreverent.

I did not steal this dream: *years later we weren't Black...we were Jews.*

I have not considered abandoning this list.

I have never ignored Africa.

Do not disdain any person.

This is the last confession I will devote to ignorance.

I do not covet innocence.

I have never pretended to be innocent.

I have not mistaken ignorance for innocence.

This is the last confession I will devote to innocence.

These confessions are (not) an experiment (in self knowledge.)

I did not steal my own image (*never tell a mirror you are white*).

These confessions are (not) meant to be read (by anyone but me).

I do not covet the woman who has no confession to make.

I have held Africa in my arms and comforted her.

I have loved Africa like a sister (daughter, lover).

This is the last confession I will devote to love.

I have not misrepresented Africa.

Africa is not my (m)other.

Honor thy father and thy mother.

I am not indebted to my own lies (for this poem).

I did not steal the conclusion (*these times begin the ending of all lies*).

I have not considered abandoning this list.

I do not expect to be forgiven (for these confessions).

I do not expect to be praised (for these confessions).

I do (not) expect to be exonerated (for these confessions).

I do not expect to be redeemed (by these confessions).

I do not expect to be reminded (of my own confessions).

This is the last confession I will devote to judgment.

I did not steal *God, the holy, just, and true.*

With truth, justice, and peace shall you judge in your gates.

I did not forget that Egypt is Africa.

I did not forget that Africa is Egypt.

I am not a slave (to ignorance).

I am not a slave (to innocence).

I will not bear false witness.

I am not a slave (to history).

I am not a slave (to my own confessions).

This is the only confession I will devote to servitude.

I have (not) mastered the art of confessing.

I did not steal this vision: *she carries Africa in her right arm.*

To the mountain which His right arm had acquired.

I would not consider Africa a metaphor.

This is the last confession I will repeat.

There is (no) power concealed in these confessions.

Do not bring us into the power of scorn.

A continent is (not) more powerful than a country.

A country is (not) more powerful than a continent.

History is (not) more powerful than memory.

Memory is (not) more powerful than history.

I do (not) understand what power has to do with these confessions.

I have not usurped a power that *will run corrupt.*

I have (not) lost my way in these confessions.

I have (not) confused the river and the sea.

I did not steal the journey: I hear talk of a Bright Star converging on Egypt.

I am the Lord, your God, who delivered you from the Land of Egypt, from the house of slavery.

I did not steal the question *what is Africa to me?*

This is the last confession I will devote to metaphor.

I do not covet the ancient metaphors (the sun from its tent in the heavens).

I have (not) forgotten the genealogy (of these confessions).

I have (not) forgotten the morphology (of these oppressions).

I have (not) forgotten the destiny (of these digressions).

I have (not) forgotten the origin (of these expressions): *Deep, deep as the river. By the river of Babylon there we sat and wept when we remembered Zion.*

This is the last confession I will devote to history.

I would not consider Africa (Egypt, Zion) a metaphor.

I would (not) recognize evil.

Compel our Evil Inclination to be subservient to You.

I would (not) recognize a criminal night.

I am (not) a sister to ignorance.

I am (not) the inventor of innocence.

I do (not) shelter madness (or mistakes).

I am (not) the author of cruelty.

I would (not) recognize Africa.

I would (not) recognize Egypt.

I would (not) know my ancestors.

I would (not) recognize slavery.

I would (not) recognize redemption.

This is the only confession I will devote to evil. Evil.

I did not steal the line *humanitarians…explorers, soldiers, mercenaries, imperialists, missionaries, adventurers*. Poets.

Mine is yours and yours is yours.

I have not considered abandoning this list.

This is the only confession I will devote to the lost confessions.

I would (not) deny that all these confessions are negative.

I did not steal this prayer: *I scarce could tell them anything of Africa, though much of my hope of Heaven.*

Thou shalt not steal.

I do not covet the sound Africa, the lyric Africa,
                          the *great dark symphony.*

I did not steal that music.

This is the last confession I will devote to theft.

These confessions are not *black as Cain.*

These confessions do not contain a graven image.

I am (not) a slave to my own exile.

You redeemed us from the house of bondage.

I despise evil.

This is the last confession I will devote to what I despise.

I can (not) trace the geography of hatred.

I can (not) configure the geometry of hatred.

I can (not) dissect the biology of hatred.

I can (not) decipher the cosmology of hatred.

I did not steal *the unhealed history*.

You shall not covet your neighbor's house.

I have (not) finished confessing.

III

Philosophy

Insomnia

It's not the war that keeps me up nights —
(There's always a war somewhere, isn't there?)

Didn't I sleep through Tempestuous May and Bloody Sunday
                    the war of rocks and conflict diamonds
                    the raid on Haiphong Harbor
                    the strafing fire at Grand Anse Beach?

Didn't I sleep through sieges at the Golden Temple and the Temple Mount
                    the attacks on Stolac and Pocitelj,
                    on Drag Yerpa, on Chimpu?

Didn't I sleep through the tanks in Tlatelolco, Asunción, Santiago
                    the kidnapping in Estelí?

More likely it's the body's demise,
my aging chemistry,
that holds sleep hostage,
one more ambushed routine.

Sometimes after a wakeful night,
I fall asleep just before day breaks —

— in my dream the sound of the sky
halved and helpless
                    wakes me.

Burial Society

They always paid attention to the dead
my (now dead) relations, *baruch ha-shem*,
may they rest in peace.
Blessing the outstretched arm,
cursing the hand of the wicked,
resuscitating family names to confuse the demons,
reviving their lost light, sundown to sundown.
Every Sabbath — an opportunity to remember.
Every festival — an occasion for mourning.

I avoided them, the dead and the living,
their martyred houses,
their burnt books,
their fugitive nights.
And if it was a sin or a crime
to say I was sick and tired
of the sins and the crimes, I'd live with it.
But I wouldn't swallow death
with every breath, every blessing.
I wouldn't pray at the altar of memory.

How they found me, I can't be certain,
their tattooed spirits stacked in heaps
on my desk. My study — a morgue —
where a thousand wounded stories
lie exposed, waiting for me
to examine, to probe
with morbid tools:
this scavenger pen,
these fresh pages,
not yet bled dry.

Perception — A Life in Philosophy

Teresa Benedicta a Cruce, OCD, née Edith Stein (1891–1942)

I. "The Problem of Empathy" – 1916

What can be left if the whole world and even the subject
experiencing it are cancelled?

Pure investigation was her answer.
Not purity: vows and veils,
the enclosure, hemp sandals on

glad, impoverished feet. Objectivity:
freedom from servitude to false
perceptions, the sin of the outwardly

perceived body. Allegiance to the Father
of phenomenology and to the spirit
of her own scholarly inclination.

II. "The Significance of Women's Intrinsic Value in National Life" – 1930

Scholarship is the realm of the most austere objectivity…as a rule,
the masculine-intellectual type predominates…However, woman
may perhaps assert her singularity…by the way she instructs…

Eight long years of longing to belong
to the two worlds that embraced, then
eluded her, the academy — closed to

women, and the cloister — closed to
converts. She was not called to
teach, but still she taught: the science

of teaching. And she lectured, first on women's
professions and later on their vocations:
help-mate, companion, mentor, mother.

III. "On the History and Spirit of Carmel" – 1935

Nor does every age give us a reign of terror during which we
have the opportunity to lay our heads on the executioner's block
for our faith and for the ideals of our Order as did the sixteen
Carmelites of Compiegne.

Chastity, poverty, obedience — finally received
behind the grille, enclosed, clothed
in the white robes and dark nights

of her new profession. Already forty-one
she was the only philosopher
in the novitiate, but not the only student

of suffering. Every member of the community
prayed for an honest burden, sought to
know salvation as obscurity, as stillness.

IV. Letter to Sr. Maria Ernst, OCD, Carmel at Cologne
Sent From the Carmel at Echt, Holland – 1941

Faith in the secret history must always strengthen us when what
we actually perceive…might discourage us.

Who among us would not grieve
the loss of family? Certainly she missed
the twenty Sisters in Cologne, but for safety's

sake she left her dear country (having long
since left her Nation). Loyalty to the Rule
can be tested anywhere. Her blood

sister Rosa followed, too, though she did
not enter the new house, or escape
when they came to take them both away.

V. Letter to the Swiss Consulate, Amsterdam
Sent from Drente-Westerbork, Barracks 36 – 1942

Enable us as soon as possible to cross the border. Our monastery
will take care of the travel expenses.

Born on the Day of Atonement,
killed on the fast of *Tisha Be-Av*
she asked, after all, to be spared,
her terse plea scribbled (*please do not*
mention that you got this) on the back
of a braver missive: *we are very calm and cheerful.*

The fire was unforgiving, consuming
even the echoes — *Gott in Himmel, Pater Noster,*
Deutschland, Deutschland, über alles.

To Count Myself Among Them

Not knowing how to treat their bodies in life is one thing.
Not knowing how to treat them in death is another. So I study:
thin fog of cloth over the flesh; twenty-four quarts; eyes
open now that there's nothing to see. I would study a map,
too, if such a thing existed — my great grandfather's grave
in Sátoraljaujhely, my grandmother's grave in Greensboro. My
great grandfather's grave in Belarus (isn't that a country now?) my
grandfather's grave in Albany. Do you remember the names
of the cemeteries? Guilford County might be as foreign to me
as Hungary. I'm not certain where my parents plan to be
buried — dust to dust, eyes open now that there's nothing
to see.

If Everything That Burns

If everything that burns to ash   (fire)

       or slackens to rest   (Sabbath)

everything that is light alone   (honey)

       or none at all   (sleep)

is a sixtieth part of something else

where are you, beloved, in this equation

       this bright wilderness   (dream)

where what cannot be counted

       wanders between this world and the next?   (prophecy)

       I make my home in Paradise

          with you.

       Your rounded thighs like jewels:

           silver, saffron, rose, and cedar.

     Your eyes:

     the only sea.

Promise me, woman who rises from the desert,

you will remember the days of our desire   in the world to come.

First Text

1

The (untranslatable) tree
Of life is every
One and
None.

2

Q: Before one, what do you count?
A: The one who is counting.

3

The vineyard, the garden, the orchard:
Where the words grew
Those worlds that were destroyed at the beginning
Destroyed at the beginning
At the beginning
At the

4

Q: To repair the unredeemed world.
A: Is that the question or the answer?

5

The primal impulse resides in the great palace of metaphor.

6

Q: The most secret of all things which is the soul.
A: Is that the answer or the question?

7

My body, this light.
This light, my skin.
Boundary that separates
The world above from the world below.

8

What is revealed is concealed until it is revealed. Until it is r-e-( )-a-l.

9

Q: What is there to fear in the *Book of Brightness?*
A: That you will enter and not emerge.

10

Black fire on white fire
      close your lips
      around the secrets
Swallow the sparks.

The Tip of the *Yud*

I can't help myself:

we're barely on our feet
to greet the Sabbath Bride,
whose invisible veil
trails two thousand years of
manly metaphors
across the threshold of the sanctuary,
and already I'm thinking about the tip of the *yud*.

I really did intend to try,
just this once,
this first Friday night
after a lifetime
of Sabbath-less weekends,
decades of wholly secular rest,
to relax my standards.
But before I've even had a chance
to loosen my grip on the ordinary day
I'm embracing this sacred lady of leisure,
opening my lips to sanctify her maker,
and the only words I can utter are
slain by the tip of the yud
again.

It's not even a good translation — "tip."
It's the edge really or perhaps the hook,
the curve of the *yud* that leans
(salaciously) toward the letter next to it,
but doesn't quite touch.
And it's a good thing, too, that abstinence,
since it's forbidden, a sin,
an unholy alliance between sounds.

Although it's not the over zealous *yud*,
but the absent *yud*,
that gave rise to "The Tip of the *Yud*,"
Judah Leib Gordon's satirical nod
to the missing *yud* that kept his fictional Bat-shu'a
a *yud*'s breath away from being free (to marry again).

     In her divorce decree
     from a husband lost at sea
     the writing was found, alas, to be
     one *yud* short.
     So she lived out her long life in misery.
     And you should know
     that Leib Gordon did not agree!
     And he makes a mockery
     of the Rabbi's decision.
     For it turns out no *yud* was really
     necessary for the name in question.

I thought he was ahead of his time,
at the turn of the century,
pre-feminism, a progressive thinker,
a true *mensch*, a champion.
Until I read about his wife, who was weak, ill,
while he ignored her.
So busy composing his diatribe
against the men who made the rules
he didn't know how sick she was.
Until I learned he told the woman (not his wife)
to whom he dedicated "The Tip of the *Yud*"
that Jewish women were luckier than most,
they shouldn't complain.
Slain by the tip of the yud,
again.

I can't explain to the woman
next to me in the pew
what I'm muttering with such disdain,
under my breath. But here I am,
at the turn of the century,
post-feminism, a progressive thinker,
chanting this virile welcome to a fantasy
even Judah Leib Gordon must have entertained,
to the sweet bride of respite and mystical union.
Suddenly I'm straining to follow
the transliteration, to hear the Rabbi,
(she, naturally, reads from the Hebrew)
waiting for this queen who reigns
every seventh day,
before I realize I've been
slain by the tip of the yud,
again.

Secondary Sources

in praise of parallelism

I keep these truths
in separate pockets:
the things I must remember
                            to dwell in myself
to dwell in myself
                        the things I must forget.

Blues in the Night

My mama don tol' me, when I was in knee pants,
my mama don tol' me, son!
Johnny Mercer, "Blues in the Night"

For my father

Nobody told me anything.

Not how to move the thumb under
the middle finger. At E, F#, Bb.
Not how to press the pedal to the floor I couldn't
reach without lifting myself full off
the seat, stretching beyond my years,
riding low the way I'd learned to push forward
on the used two-wheeler that carried me on my paper route
and to the corner store for an egg cream. Extra seltzer.

Nobody told me anything.

Not how to avoid bruises, reprisals, justice transposed:
Please, Harry, oh God, please stay away from his hands,
my mother pleaded while my father beat me for
beating the boy who called me "dirty Jew," "dirty kike sissy,"
after school on the corner of Highland and Grove.

Nobody told me anything.

Not how to move through a cycle of fifths
translating impulse and urge to essential pitch
while my classmates played basketball and man-about-town
and trailed unskilled fingers in clumsy half-steps
under the smooth, narrow hems of girls named Doris or Eileen.

Not how to leave the downbeat in the Village,
head uptown — graduate school — where the measure of success
was not like any good, cool, hep cat's way to swing.
They were teaching me to be the teacher, when all along I thought
that rhythm was the only mentor anyone would need.

Nobody told me anything.

Not how to want that teaching degree
when nature improvised on what we'd left unplanned
in our two-room, tenth floor walk-up,
north end of Riverside Drive — twin girls— all song and spectacle,
a new motif, nevertheless, diapers and doctors' bills.

Not how to keep working double time
when later there was a third (another girl)
and then a perfect fourth (a boy),
and instead of jam sessions, an endless
progression of brides and grooms, bar mitzvah boys
with sweaty palms and the promise of sideburns,
golden anniversaries, retirement jamborees,
and two dozen variations of "Norwegian Wood,"
the bride's cousin fancies herself a singer.

Nobody told me anything.

Not how to keep time with teenagers in the Age of Aquarius,
or with aging parents in steady decline.
The pace was without reprieve,
a pattern of unoriginal modulations as I
shuffled from one scale of expectation to the next.

Sometimes, it's true, for brief intervals
between unbroken lines, a relentless forward motion,
I knew a moment of delight and imprecision,
dutiful fingers wild and savvy and on their own.

Nobody told me anything.

Not how to distinguish the timeless nights (and days),
after the second, the third surgeries,
when through a liquid arc of sensation I heard
a trio of percussive constancy:
heart monitor, respirator, the sighs, short and measured,
of my wife, our grown children, in turns,
at the foot of the bed.

Not how to articulate a desire for silence
after the heartless ensemble of artificial
beats and pulses that accompanied me in ICU,
high pitched sound and light show, meant to keep in check
the possibility of internal syncopation.

Nobody told me anything.

Not how to sustain a note of confidence,
the stamina for those first diminished weeks and months
out of the hospital,
plans and wishes as shriveled and depressed
as this old man's chest,
ragged breastbone resting, in pieces, on a muscle
that used to reside in the shoulder,
unsure if my arm, hand, fingers, would remember themselves
in this new configuration,
if the body would perform the unadorned routines
it had practiced for more than six decades.

Nobody told me anything.

Not how to learn not to be young,
transcribe to thought every theme and inclination,
when, like everyone, I had always
played-it-by-ear. Not how to reach, finally, again,
across octaves of habit and obligation
toward the primitive music of the self.

IV

The Jewish Fake Book

The Jewish Fake Book

The first Jewish Fake Book — 212 songs for every possible occasion, selected by the world's foremost authority on Jewish music.

Velvel Pasternak
Tara Publications Catalogue, 1997

(1)

It's part of the trade, if you're a musician. They give you a fake book: just the key signatures, D major for a lively Romanian *frailich*, D minor for a soulful Russian *sher*, a modest eight-bar melody, the chord progressions. If you know the difference between an augmented fourth and a diminished fifth, you're set. You follow along with the others and you make it up as you go. You don't have to learn every tune for every gig. Nobody expects you to. You play every number as if you came into this world grasping the horn in your fist, the entire repertoire hibernating in the cells of your fingertips, and nobody's the wiser. Sometimes the bandleader says "two-four time, don't get sluggish, but be careful not to rush." So you know you'd better not make the eighth notes too *legato* or too staccato, but nice and even, maybe spring off the quarter notes a little bit, as if you were curious to see what happens next. Or maybe the drummer gets it in her head that a nice old-fashioned *hora* would sound better with a back beat, and sure, you get a little flustered at first, but after a few reckless measures, you've got the hang of it, and it's as if you've always played "*Hava Nagila*" as though Chuck Berry had written it. And believe it or not, I've even heard renditions of songs as famous as, say, "*Bei Mir Bist Du Sheyn*," where everybody is so busy trying to figure out a clever, original harmony that all of a sudden, there's no melody. That's when music, for me, is the most like the rest of life. Once in a while the fake book is just plain wrong and it sounds like you and the accordion are locked in mortal combat. A completely unacceptable dissonance. Unless the F sharp in that second triplet was meant to be an F natural. So, on occasion, you have to ignore the instructions, play the F natural, and pretty soon the accordion player smiles and slides easily into a long generous *glissando*, just to show you she approves. You're faking it — but that's the way it's supposed to be.

(2)

But to be a Jew, to be a Jew they hand you the whole world
(*die ganze veld*) in a book. And then another, and another, and
another, all to be certain you understand the first one. They tell
you everything, I mean everything you have to learn, to know
by heart — what to eat, what to wear, when to work, when not
to, what to say when the new moon rises, that gracious crown
over the heavens. They tell you how to shovel the dirt over a
newly dug grave; what color tablecloth to lay beneath a
Sabbath feast; how to divide a loaf of bread; how many feet
you may walk on waking from the place where you slept to
the place where you'll wash your hands. They tell you not to
weave, or tear, or thresh, or scrape, or trap, or winnow; not to
knead or grind, or sift, or spin; not to build a fire or put one
out on Saturday. They tell you when to bend your knees,
recline to the left, lift yourself up on your toes. Do keep salt on
the altar of your table; always wash the right hand before the
left; and after seven years, forgive a debt. To a mourner advise
a prayer for peace; to celebrate a first-born son, and only a son,
say *yes, yes*, you'll redeem him and offer up five silver *shekels*.
Learn the laws of modesty, of mingled threads. Beware of
things unclean: a fish with neither scales nor fins; a reptile that
slinks, guileful sorcerer across your path, a woman when she
bleeds. You must know that it is men who are required, by
law, to procreate. So, of course, a childless widow may
remarry, but only if for her new mate she takes her late
husband's brother.

(3)

As for music, it is, I knew it all along, sin and celebration —
Solomon's undoing and the "Song of Ascents," seduction and
sanctification, divine inspiration and the heathen's noisy
godlessness. It is the sea parting, the glass shattering, the
harvest ripening, our enemies scheming. It is my heart striking
the tempo to accompany the question: what is true, what is
true, what is true, what is true?

Notes

Sacrilege   The quotation from Edmond Jabès is found in *From the Book to the Book. An Edmond Jabès Reader*, translated from the French by Rosemarie Waldrop (Hanover, New Hampshire: Wesleyan University Press, 1991).

Guide of the Perplexed   The citation from Marc-Alain Ouaknin is found in *The Burnt Book. Reading the Talmud*, translated from the French by Llewellyn Brown (Princeton, New Jersey: Princeton University Press, 1995).

Other Egypts   I am indebted to Ellen Frankl's work *The Five Books of Miriam: A Woman's Commentary on the Torah* (New York: G. P. Putnam's Sons, 1996) for this phrase.

One Hundred and Forty-Seven Negative Confessions   The ancient African document "One Hundred and Forty-Seven Negative Confessions" is identified as a model for the *Ten Commandments in The African Origins of Modern Judaism: From Hebrews to Jews*, by Jose V. Malcioln (Trenton, New Jersey: Africa World Press, Inc., 1996). Text fragments are from the work of: Ai, Toi Derricotte, Countee Cullen, C.S. Giscombe, Robert Hayden, June Jordan, Langston Hughes, Nathaniel Mackey, Alberto Torres Pereira, Sonia Sanchez, Reginald Shepherd, Melvin B. Tolson, Phyllis Wheatley, and James Monroe Whitfield.

Beyond Uranium   Several phrases are derived from the letters and diaries of Lise Meitner as quoted in *Lise Meitner. A Life in Physics* by Ruth Ellen Sime (Berkeley: University of California Press, 1996).

In the *Tzitzit* Laboratory   *Tzitzit* are the fringes on traditional prayer shawls, as described in the Torah, *Numbers*

15:38-40. *Tekhelet* is the unique shade of blue of these fringes, said to have been made from snails' ink.

On the Second Page   Information about the alteration and obliteration of Arabic names and the physical landscape is found in *Sacred Landscape: The Buried History of the Holy Land Since 1948* by Meron Bienvenisti, translated by Maxine Kaufman-Lacusta (Berkeley, California: University of California Press, 2000). Bienvenisti quotes official documents of the "Committee for the Designation of Place Names in the Negev Region."

The Wrong Law   The concept of the wrong law is derived from *Fatal Error. The Miscarriage of Justice that Sealed the Rosenberg's Fate* by Joseph H. Sharlitt (New York: Charles Scribner's Sons, 1989). The citation from Ethel Rosenberg's letter and other phrases are found in *We Are Your Sons*, by Robert and Michael Meeropol (Boston: Houghton Mifflin, 1975).

Perception — A Life in Philosophy   Citations from Edith Stein are from *On the Problem of Empathy*, translated by Waltraut Stein (Washington, D.C.: ICS Publications, 1989); *Edith Stein's Woman*, translated by Freda May Oben (Washington, D.C.: ICS Publications, 1987); *The Hidden Life. Hagiographic Essays, Meditations, and Spiritual Texts*, translated by Waltraut Stein (Washington, D.C.: ICS Publications, 1992); *Self Portrait in Letters*, translated by Josephine Koeppel (Washington, D.C.: ICS Publications, 1993). Biographical information is derived from *Edith Stein. Life in a Jewish Family 1891-1916*, translated by Josephine Koeppel (Washington, D.C.: ICS Publications, 1986); *Edith Stein*, by Sister Teresia de Spiritu Sancto, O.C.D., translated by Cecile Hastings and Donald Nicholl (New York: Sheed and Ward, 1952); *Edith Stein. A Biography*, by Waltraud Herbstrith, translated by Father Bernard Bonowitz, OCSO (San Francisco: Harper & Row, 1985).

If Everything That Burns   Phrases inspired by and derived from the *Song of Songs* are found in *TANAKH. A New Translation of the Holy Scriptures According to the Traditional Hebrew Text* (Philadelphia: The Jewish Publication Society, 1985). The last verse contains language from "Song of Farewell" by Judah Halevi in *The Penguin Book of Hebrew Verse*, edited and translated by T. Carmi (New York: Penguin Books, 1981).

The Tip of the *Yud* The title is from the lengthy narrative poem of the same name, *"Kozo shel Yud,"* by Judah Leib Gordon (1830-1892), which refers to the laws for writing sacred texts, as explained in the *Talmud* (*Menahot* 29b). No complete English translation of the poem exists; several stanzas have been translated by Michael Stanislawski in his book *For Whom Do I Toil? Judah Leib Gordon and the Crisis of Russian Jewry* (New York: Oxford University Press, 1988).

Blues in the Night "Blues in the Night," lyrics by Johnny Mercer, music by Harold Arlen (Remick Music Corporation, 1941).

The Jewish Fake Book Tara Publications publishes an international fake book of Jewish songs, *The Jewish Fake Book* (Cedarhurst, NY: Tara Publications, 1997). A fake book is a simple musical score consisting of a melody line and basic chords. Experienced musicians create arrangements and improvise from this text.

Other Titles From
ELIXIR PRESS

Assignation at Vanishing Point
   Jane Satterfield
   0-9709342-9-7 • $13

Running the Voodoo Down
   Jim McGarrah
   0-9709342-8-9 • $13

Drag
   Duriel E. Harris
   1-932418-00-8 • $14

Nomadic Foundations
   Sandra Meek
   0-9709342-3-8 • $13

Flow Blue
   Sarah Kennedy
   0-9709342-5-4 • $13

Monster Zero
   Jay Snodgrass
   0-9709342-6-2 • $13

Circassian Girl
   Michelle Mitchell-Foust
   0-9709342-2-X • $13

Distance From Birth
   Tracy Philpot
   0-9709342-1-1 • $13